# DIMENSIONS

## HUES OF A HEART

## SHASHI

To a happy soul in here!

# Contents

# Contents

# Contents

# Prologue

We feel ecstatic, euphoric and contented and at the same time we get those adrenaline rushes, fears, insecurity and ambiguity about ourself. When we see the world we see it through the lens of perception, insight and our own opinions. We are sceptic about this hoar world and sometimes elevated by its beauty and pleasures. All of these poems open up to some feelings, certain happenings and few ideals.

Pardon all the flaws and feel the flow of this heart. I am grateful to everyone!

# 1. Night

Whole city enraptured in darkness,
a full moon with the clumsy feel of happiness,
dazzling stars, adoring dark sky,
tired birds flying upon the bay;
Blowing breeze carrying away,
my breath along the beach,
waves hitting the shore, halting the souls,
making them forget their fouls;
Salty air,
embracing with care,
curing fearlessly monstrous contagion,
my walk under the starlight with moon, as my companion;
Night that showed me the light,
rocks now are pebbles tomorrow,
rivers due time lose their might,
in diligence to the sea they vow;

# 2. My apologies, dear heart

Few moments hold you back,
clinging on to goodness sack,
you try to avoid,
but how? it fills your void;
Hey little one,
my little heart,
I made you shutter,
beat and moan;
Teased you with various pain,
pinched you in vain,
I was so insane,
you were her main;
"I'm sorry I held you back",
made you away from light pack,
held your innocence,
with my common sense;
Blackened your love,
with my logic,
but now, with time I saw,
It's all 'miracle and magic';
My little one,
I know you are longing for some,
of one,

I send you my apologies, little one;
Realised my ego was crankiest,
of utter waste,
but, your ago was the happiest
filled with wisdom;
I'm sorry
I owe you pleasure
I owe you allure
I owe you feelings
- my apologies
'From Brain'.

# 3. Spirituality

Sweet redolence,
calming fragrance
of the most spiritual incense,
building up a calm spiritual sense;
Mind is in ignorance,
winding up for the commence
of the questions,
what is 'spirituality' and its essence?
I closed my eyes,
let the breeze hit my strands,
my soul ayes,
to reach the inner corner through the colourful bands;
I feel something which I never felt,
"my ears are shut,
all I can feel is my heart melt"
peace is rushing in my veins cult;
Chaos of the world outside,
is turned into the musical slide,
something in us abide,
to leave everything, run behind peace and reside;
All these realisation,
was by a sweet sensation,
in a seconds of the time's narration,

this aroma's creation;

I closed my eyes again,

to flush my lungs with the essence of the incense fragrance!

• 5 •

# 4. Green

When I gazed around,
within the natural breeze;
the place around me is clamouring in green,
with chilled calm of blooming blues, hues;
Hushing busy hours of urban lands,
busy and tiry colour of different dyes;
uhh, coming in to the drapes of plants,
beautiful painting to our watery eyes;
Terrifyingly tired eyes tearing the troubles,
clearing their eyes in the view of greens and pebbles;
little tiny creatures carrying their food for cold,
little playful butterflies galloping around the bulgy flowers
with the nectar of gold;
How foolish flesh we were missing all these,
the happiest life around us, for the life of stress;
may be, we forgot the life of peace
ended up running in to the mess;
That warmth of natural farms,
being a smallest creature, of this whole life;
I would have gave up my life to be hammered in to smash,
now, "every moment will replenish again as a flowering fresh"!

# 5. Queen

She is queen,
to know this I was keen;
she owns kingdom,
she owns wealth and health;
Majesty of her beauty,
but not free from cruelty;
She have everything more than suffice,
still her freedom is full of ice;
Everyday fire burns within her,
every night desires get suppressed in her;
Royalty and richness never showed her,
the way to happiness ever;
She have her own 'obsessions',
she have her own preventions,
merely because she is a woman,
she is under a man's 'precautions'!

# 6. Haunting terrors

I got a jerk in my head,
a sharp sneaky voice was heard,
someone screaming in my ear,
struggling! opened my eyes due to adrenaline fear;
It was calm out there,
soft breeze was making drapes dance bare,
cosy in moon's care
huff! it was a nightmare
Cold air struck my ear,
chills went down my spine,
my hands were still clutching the sheets of fear,
rewinding the stories of syne;
Everything was like a play,
as if characters were forged to slay,
everyone commencing near me,
calling me..."come come come"!
I was turning my back to all
I was vague, fetish, unrealized, about to fall
huff,
it is not a bluff;
I looked up to search the moon,
he was on head, pure serene
his tenderness gave me boon,

gave me to hold on a cane;
Took a deep breath, flushing my lungs with air
holding him tight,
his hands caressing my hair,
I closed my eyes tight, fighting the past!

# 7. Confusion

Confession is the only way,
to clear the confusion
comfort doesn't matter when,
there is no manifestation
Yes, confusions create chock-a-blocks,
when brain gets sacked,
in the misunderstanding sacks,
with the perception being tacked;
Come away from that peep hole!
make an effort to acknowledge it as a whole
as you do, satisfactions will be shown in your smile,
a little thought will yield you to a better while;
Clear off all the confusion,
look into all sides of the perception.

# 8. Northern lights

Desire to mum my eyes by northern lights,
ego surrendering sights;
fearing the fright away,
far from where I stay;
Place where suffering and slay,
had never been on a play;
spirit pot being made from color of the sky,
vibrant as to make the earth shy;
I wanna be there,
under the moonlight's way;
my eyes capturing the beautiful lights,
within those warm arms, 'just lay';
The northern lights,
desires from the heights
of the hearts,
to catch those colours;

# 9. Dear, love

Your presence makes the moon to shy away,

your tenor makes my heart sway,

my folly, I never realized your tunes of trust

my eyes were fogged off by the mist;

My heart gave me various cues

when beautiful hues came with you denigrating blues;

You enchanted your spell by chance,

by choice "bless my eyes with your glance";

O beloved! in my tiny life your arrival,

made me love the instance, you became my prior from my rival

rustic tunes of music,

and your brightness made the moon sick,

"hold my hand to the infinite" beyond those stars

admiring the beauty of the Earth from Mars;

# 10. Monsoon

A valiant warrior,

with sparkling lightning spear,

against his conspirator,

slicing the cloud to tear;

Peace after the war,

victory of the victorious "Rain the tsar"

sound of silence with its essence,

calming melancholy condolence;

Death can't be held back,

sack of the almight is on his back;

keeping all the track,

ticking off the Earth with his check

It was the sunrise,

new rays in their prise

brought a happiest surprise

full of life size;

The drizzling cold sound,

of drifted heaven from the cloud;

Monsoon showers have started to bloom,

weaving threads of life in the loom;

maiden start for the damp day,

with mist hovered valiant vibrant sky;

peace and solitude makes hearts fly,

changing smiles popping out from a lone cry;
Few temptations of the heart arise,
to enjoy every bit of this 'paradise',
ahh! craving to sip hot tea in the balcony,
and crispiest corn with dearest company;
Whoa!
Let's welcome this weather
and clear the hatred from the clutter,
"Let's love to the fullest"!

# 11. Scams

A dishonest fraud,
due to an ugly greed;
and a tempt to be found,
as a richest and poverty freed;
secured behind governments security,
clever clutches of cupidity;
behind the public eyes,
on the public's assets;
Vijay mallya to Nirav modi, crossed the shores
everyone leading a lavish life as the ruler of ghor;
carrying and absconding from the country,
coal scam, 2G spectrum scam and bofors all vary;
"Why to shut our mouth"!
when it's our money,
we earned it,
we paid it as tax;
Expectations of development
was spent in the sea of scandals;
money is being looted in scams
then why to shut our mouths?
years have been passed,
corruption is becoming the jewels of the people,
why law, on this issue is not being stressed?

morality is being shed as maple;
The scams,
order must be changed.
Strict laws must be made.
Beautiful India is yet to be carved!

# 12. You

A quick reflection,
to acknowledge our 'minds interpretation';
When, we don't even think
background bearing of our mind,
never stops to link
the ink,
Why, even when we ignore
it comes to be the fore,
when we love to be fire,
we end up feeling unable to bear
When, we cry for loneliness
whole world sticks to us,
Heart swearing for a companion,
brain reminding us about compulsion;
We feel it, we have wings to fly yet,
dependence, is what hindering our dreams to meet,
we beg for solitude,
we beg to shape my own attitude
We never want to be parted,
we try to get stonehearted,
but our tears melt it unaffected,
Yes, only we can change our life & only we can do it for our self!

# 13. Karma

Kala, time, moment,
changes with the flow of scent;
descended with the world,
'Guardian' as being told;
Every second, every minute, every is hour,
is sweet and sour;
what we do today, gets repaid tomorrow
all our deeds are in a row;
You harm mother Earth,
she will harm you;
Face the heat of her wrath,
you will definitely lose your breath;
Above and beneath,
it's all petrified;
surreptitiously whole life will surrender,
under her thunder!
Karma; a cycle of good and bad,
"yin and yong
happy and sad"
all in a cycle of on a wheel of Life!

# 14. Meadow

In this mind blogging meadow,

I am the smallest flower dancing to the winds flow,

I am shook by the lightning sparks,

and took away to heaven when the butterfly lurks;

My heart if is filled with feel of 'peppy'

and my dreams for nectar may feel silly ;

I'm just the smallest one,

hopping to the winds tune;

It was finally the time to cherish,

and make my art astonish,

as the seconds are sliding on,

my petals are falling off;

My petals are getting experiences,

leaving back their traces,

ambitions getting fulfilled,

life with some compliments;

I have not lost my petals,

they fell off from me

"to bear the sweetest fruit of life"!

# 15. Cleopatra

Egyptian pharaoh,

queen with her beauty as her weapon;

Incestuous; she was married to her two young brothers,

which neither bothered her nor gutted her;

Capable ruler with competent brains,

and an eye capturing beauty;

the great roman emperor 'Julius Ceaser' captured the Egypt,

within his clutches with his might feisty;

In that captivity and time of trouble,

Cleopatra as goddess of 'Aphrodite',

alluring eyes and lithe body made him feeble;

he embraced her to his eternity and filled his appetite;

But, perished in the hands of "Brutus; the conspirator"

Second triumvirate started,

'Mark antony' was stated,

as a paramour, illicit Cleopatra's dearest partner;

Both couple fought actium war for love,

made the world low,

by killing themselves in war,

rather being beheaded somewhere far;

Cleopatra!

clever ruler,

contented beauty

Nefarious, Notorious Hathor,
for love and power!

# 16. Fear

Fear, is something we don't wanna hear
in that black space of heart,
lies a small section apart,
holding the new start;
Where dark is reminiscent,
and, fear is lot more than sufficient,
this makes us nervous,
this makes us conscious;
Nightmares, though ignored
Yet, grabs a lot of care
"Blood pumps through the body",
I'm there standing lonely
With an unwelcomed guest,
who is there with a quest?,
there is something,
which is advancing;
It's my negative thoughts,
discreet part of mine,
It's negativity,
Yes, it's the demon in me!

# 17. Optimism

The most optimistic dreams,
are definitely with no 'fears'
inevitable phases,
Stable mind can bring some changes;
Little steps seems to be significant,
yet, too little to become a commitment;
little things of our life made us smile,
Vast desires in our hearts compile;
A picture of that contented life draws across my eyes,
My brain pinches me up reminding,
this needs a hard work of seas
which will be soon commencing;
A terror finds a place in my heart
"Will my dreams of life,
can become into a failure knife"
Efforts must be like sweet tart;
If I have dreamt about it,
I cannot sleep peacefully till I hit it;
Sheer determination will be my only,
Inspiration!

# 18. Beach

Dear beach,

you made me search,

for the love, with our conscious mind

in the soulful sand;

Long stretch of sand, made us mad,

and took us to the goddess "Venus's land";

we made it reach

to its zenith, held the bow of cupid on it's catch;

Fishing nets made me curious,

O dear thee beauty is prius,

you made us propitious,

'Oracle's spell' of our future has to be auspicious;

Green garden's quench,

aroma of chocolate on skin as a sketch,

ecstatic etch,

beyond every hitch;

Dear beach,

"Our happiness in you was like waves you outreach"!

# 19. Tears

Yes, I am a tear,
On that verge of a soulful eye,
I am the one expressing the cry,
shedding the heart's fear;
I am in your heart
when, no more pain can be bore
when, you need that warmest supporting cuddle
but the only thing I can create is a puddle,
I am like the variation of various colours,
I am not only an expression of grief,
also a drip of relief,
from success stories to the tense of failures;
Satisfactory drops of cheer,
A freckle of frightening fear,
I am the tearful tears;
Yes, I'm the 'You' trying to bear;

# 20. Summers

In the hottest heat of summers,
a sweetest pour of mango-showers;
warm endings of the evenings,
with cosiest welcomings;
Sky filled with clouds,
and rain formed from the moulds;
barren and weathered rocks
eager to caress damp folks;
Aura filled with the delightful aura
made the heart sprang to spring
first rain dry ridicule sarcasm,
filled the souls with enthusiasm;
First rain,
freed life from lifeless strain!

# 21. War

War,
Arena of death, for mere person's ego and wrath;
Calm and fierce sound of 'Shankh',
makes the world sink in the bloody ink;
Shattered and slayed bodies,
smeared with patriotism and rotting with flies;
Dark woven aura of welcoming death in home,
to carter the wishes of some;
Why can't people be empathetic?
homes lay incomplete in all eyes,
listening to all the "merry and sympathetic",
trying to recover in their destructed worlds;
Why such violence?
For Land? For Money? For Power?
why so materialistic?
when soul is unceasingly non materialistic;
Love, humanism, emotions and feelings are not for your life
but for your soul;
Life endangering games are not fair,
"O you dear Crowned head".

# 22. Time

Master of this world,

tackles the path of life's fold;

keeper of past, present and future hold,

best traitor of this humanistic world;

Runs around the globe,

still in a person's lobe,

it's on its best,

if you reject its value; definitely you will regret your fate;

Once lost you are a loser,

but, you cannot get hold of it either;

prevention is it's better utilisation,

ruler of this universe, can't buy even with a full purse;

'Life's builder and a good guilder',

Respect the clock else your life will be a chock-a-block,

Adhere to your assignments,

feel those fulfilments;

Else, with time your future will be on your complaints,

It's time,

Every second, every hour;

It's sweet and sour, be on its favour!

# 23. Vibe

A cold breeze blowing ,
through the fragile leaves of a tree
Damp and cloudy atmosphere,
sphere of gloom everywhere;
Eager hearts to fill their heart with good vibes,
aura made their faces fill with smiles,
in this heat of pandemic,
tensed tones of this demonic;
When whole life is in danger,
little relief was eager;
change in climate
brought little hopes for better fate;
It's not too late yet,
little changes are yet to be meet,
when everyone is ready to cope up,
hopes can pull us up!

# 24. Rapture by rain

A moment of magnificence,
reminding its every significance;
giving every life a chance,
to feel the feeling of soulful suffice;
An epiphany of this view being ethereal, which only an inner
eye can see;
a spiritual vibration of the rain sounding- "AUM", which only
the inner ears can hear;
when this drop touches a bare hand,
one could sense the sensual silence;
When rain cleanses your aura,
heart thrives for sizzling hot food,
to gulp everything, a big tummy stood,
can sow as well as erase an era;
Rain a spiritual, paradisiacal heaven,
bringing smiles on men;
when?
when rain was on head ,
leading you to the humble happiness ahead!

# 25. Chess

A game of pawn,

miniature war;

till the dawn,

till you reach the king from far air, on white mare;

Chess,

may make mind a mess;

you can be the master with your cleverness,

It's the war of your mind and you must confess it;

Intelligence mace,

traquillity face;

it's a race,

where your mind has to ace;

Black and white,

win and lose at your sight;

death of a pawn known for its might,

one who is on the kings left;

Army of two kingdoms,

retreating for war,

saving lives of hundreds,

and preventing the world from char;

Interaction with intelligence,

above the destruction fence,

you will win it with 'no kill';

This is the chess, a game of real life;

# 26. Constance

Constance
in a phase of life,
where, my life does symbolize lute,
mind filled with confusion;
and my brain bulb with a fused one,
I don't know, I have just lost my ad arbitrium
like, a girl with no enthusiasm
It's my passion, not just mere fashion
I neither want to get hold of any
nor, to lose any but just want
what I love, in many!
All my sparkling ideas have lost their shine,
like, no god in shrine
I'm like a warrior
but, with no armour
I do have notions, but not a single soul to support my
petitions
It's my love to portray my dreams as fancy
but, without my notice for others it's just
'The inconstancy'
How can I start the sail, where I'm not the sailor
It's my life, It's my voyage
in this vast sea, for seagulls,

I may not be savage,
In the swirl of sand a lone pyramid stands by,
in the pool of ideas, I want to that pyramid
where I can be my life's lid!
"These are not the words of wisdom,
These are the scribbling for freedom"!

# 27. Night

It's night, it's winter
cold winds have frozen the thunder,
surrounded by damp and dismal,
gloom in the warm cosy cover;
Not a single leaf on a tree,
behind the bars birds are not free;
everything is still the same,
everything sounds eerie;
Moon is glowing with the charm,
enjoying grass on the tunes of wind in the farm;
its not the end,
it's the life you lend;

# 28. Hand

Embellishment of beauty,
astonishment for its softness;
knitted by the ages of kindness,
holds the hands of the needed,
joins hands for blessings,
shakes hands with the same,
and bless the other hands;
Hard and torn off,
due to lack of work offs;
The hands that sculpt,
hands that sow,
hands that create,
hands that protects,
are the hands of humanity,
adorned by creativity and,
love of captivity;
"Hands the hues of our work,
Hard work"!

# 29. Terrorism

Al-Qaeda, ISIL, ISIS,

and lot more to create destruction of peace,

having roots from US invasion on the middle east,

vacuum of power created perfect leisure to develop terrorist caste;

9/11 attack on WTO,

Osama bin laden's plan for demolition,

rise of Jihadists,

lack of religious intolerance and government's interference;

Our nation, was suffered and is suffering from this 'black world',

26/11-2008 attacks,

endless death and loss curled,

creating havoc and panics;

It needs the whole nation to be united,

and call for the war of infinite,

to spread peace and tranquillity all over the world,

harmony yet to be unfurled;

# 30. Hope

I woke up cursing the sun,

feeling extremely low,

pain makes my heart moan,

watered my negativity with my grief, which I did sow;

I am still locked in my room,

enthusiast world out stings me like chaos,

pricks and thorns shedding blood and gloom,

I feel deserted finding the oasis;

bed hugs me tight,

weeping like a baby, I'm afraid;

running behind something, I forgot light,

"hopes brings pain and gain" as said;

I woke up, filled myself with optimistic hope,

with my life elsewhere lost, hope please cope!

"dear brain, don't get tired by the hitches,

you can come up

# 31. My realm

In the realm of this unrealistic world,
clattering sound of dancing windows,
on the tune of wind,
air is being gushed out to shout;
Tiny little damp birds on a branch,
gazing at ineffable aura,
blinking eyes in awe,
like a blooming flower in a cave;
Dry chapped out sheets of eternal love,
dancing on rain,
out of its hive,
forgetting all the pain;
It's me being mine and,
about to shine!

# 32. Feel it.

Pause,
Listen to my words,
feel it, sense it and vibe it out;
tie the emotions in peaceful cords;
When I opened my eyes,
under the moon light sky,
stars, beyond my count mounted on their chariot,
sparkling like Christmas light.
Whole sphere is in my eyes reflection,
busy hustling city life, calm in its own cocoon country side,
trees with their own shade,
uprising hills jumping towards the sky, gave me chills;
Solitude stole my soul,
pleasant plethora of joy in my heart,
vast world made epiphany hit me,
There is hell lot of world out, don't define yourself in your
count!

# 33. Subconscious!

Materialistic body, a vehicle
of non-materialistic soul;
within subconscious mind, every lie of our life is in shackle,
running away from the conscious coul;
When truth is deep in you, you boon
as embodied in your subconscious mind;
your subconscious faith will be the truth soon,
search! what is in you, you have to find;
Watch eye, Conscious mind
allowing the flowering blossoms of faith,
drain into your subconscious mind;
enough to breakthrough your death;
So ecstatic, powerful and pure,
your beliefs will get fulfilled for sure;
Your faith can change your fate,
everything depends on your mind's state;
Make your thoughts seep into
your subconscious mind;
Make them strong to endure anything,
feel the suffice in everything;

# 34. Childhood

Life that we cherish, life beyond fence,

all we had was fun in the innocence;

open vast land,

building the castle in sand;

clinging onto iron beams,

longing-ness to play all the games,

changing our names,

for flames;

Waiting desperately for 5'0 clock,

running out to play,

just like the freed flock

of birds from the cage, on to their way;

That was our real lovehood,

when we all tapped our tables for food;

scaring all the people by 'bow'

cartoons made us, "wow!";

Bedtime stories made us sleep,

getting beaten up for homework made us weep;

our mind was in shell of innocence,

with no menace;

Love for all was like our trait,

our smiles were our fate;

our fight was for candies,

dearing our intense fantasies;
Again, we want that life,
life of no stress and anxiety;
Without any fear,
caressing with care;

# 35. It's heavy

It's heavy
and rainy,
it's different,
yet eloquent;
Various paths ahead,
I know my path
but I don't know if my path will make me win this math,
as a lead;
I shed everything behind,
destiny please guide,
dear life please glide
smoothly pushing all the worries behind;
That life, life I desire
life I admire
laughter engulfed around,
peaceful and sound;
It's chaos it's loud
but there is our proud,
rainy clouds,
eyes with dreams aloud;
My eyes are heavy,
but my brain is still dreamy;
rocking on my chair,

staring upon the sky and it's starry share;
I want it,
I want my path to welcome it;
hopes! please make this true
bring colours out of this blue;
It feels burden,
I feel tired,
I want to just hide in my den,
but, I am not burned yet!
I'm still a flame,
pleading the destiny to choose my path
I don't want any blame,
because promptly I want to win this math!

# 36. Heart

Heart,
a purest creation art,
It's sweet and tart,
coziness in the cart,
affection from this part;

we accept what we have done
we know what we have gone,
all through this life's wave
a bright jewel of our body's cave;
You know, as of now
and in the the times to come,
just feel, you are pure by heart and soul,
and you will never make yourself a foul!

# 37. You can!

Everything will be still,

till it comes from your will;

To overcome the clutches of being mentally ill,

and the nightmares of butcher coming to kill;

You may feel, nothing is in your hand,

your hopes and your soul are there for you to stand;

To bring smiles on your face with a wand,

and to make you strong like a tad;

You are your ambiance,

you are your future stance,

you have to hold your lance,

and you have to leap forward to face;

In this mace,

enjoy every ace;

You aren't alone in this race,

trying to figure out your place;

Come out dear,

you deserve peace;

Something which will make you feel better,

fresh air, and light in you will make you feel lighter;

You can,

you definitely can dare to cure yourself,

to uncover your happy self, turning pages of a book in the
shelf;

# 38. Dawn

• 49 •

Sun was still hidden behind the cloud's might,
rain drops in a fight,
to hit the earth,
smearing land with new birth;
Peeping from the dark dusky clouds,
sending love moulds,
lucrative for the farmers yield,
dawn's wield;
A drop was detached from dark doom of clouds,
fragrance of the aura, from dry winds to melodious tunes,
drizzling, escaping from the smoke of chimney fumes,
paradise of earthy perfumes;
Feels pathetic for the attention gave on pity problems,
this journey of a drop from fight to a tranquil sight brought
hope emblems;

# 39. Women and wings

Tender tired rays of sun,
setting in the west;
strong enough to pierce the heart,
as a piece of an art;
God Apollo's chariot,
riot of goodness,
message of that non-resistance,
towards dishonest movements;
Far down here,
it's an abode of good and bad,
yet bad is becoming the fair,
big dad of the good;
Lies, pain, torture, disrespectfulness and lack of morality,
making life at the verge to its fragility;
making Earth lose its ability,
lacking its life compatibility;
making everyone wonder,
if I had wings I would have been that bird,
far away from the city crowd;
writing my own life, where I am the ink;
Violence is weaving India's that carpet,
where all the misery are hidden;
fear, chaos and confusion as life's pet,

it's the dark doom of the world forbidden;

close your eyes,

recall your cause,

revive all your deeds,

Fly, just fly!

# 40. Fear of missing out

World is so vast
sometimes we feel lost,
till when will you be frost,
come-on let's sort;
Tiniest sand grain
has its own prominence
it has the power to refrain
its significance;
For one, everything maiden
in this beautiful meadow, it will be none
if you don't come out of your den
to realise your music and your tone;
A long way
green lustrous leaves sway
butterfly clinging on those leaves alone
'unknown' of how many acknowledge its beauty of bringing
the floral colours in this green zone;
Beauty of exclamation,
little things bring the contemplation,
need a pinch of self-confidence
and a lot of perseverance;
Uncertainty is certain
take a deep breath, feel the tranquillity; you can come out of

your ambiguity curtain.

# 41. Hues of a heart

Blues of a dark heart,

far away from your sight;

makes you fright,

agony adds to its weight;

Some-things to make your head light,

past memories of your pleasure as your might;

clutches of blues were never caught,

as you had a flare to fight;

Blue's and red's clutch your life extremely tight,

yet,

some feelings can make your gloom into glee, as a Sunday feast;

happiness and the big hard success chest;

You may have to take a quest,

soon everyone will raise their cup on your toast,

You may be froze by frost,

but, your inner fire will melt it;

# 42. Wind inclined

Breeze embracing my free hair,
making them fly,
soul clasped on those free strands
touching the sky;
A caress of hot liquid
on my dry throat,
waves of soft wind
made me float;
Flowery essence in the aura,
and that fragrance of mud! heart melt,
the warmth in the cold rains which I felt,
cherished it more than the pandora;
Sound of this wind,
swirling in my mind,
what is yet to find,
when this sound can cure the wound;
Sound of this wind,
made hearts inclined,
to the goodness of wined,
and the humanity lined!

# 43. Cyclone

The sound fears you,
the climate hardens you;
creator of destruction,
till it feels the satisfaction;
Intensive pressure gradient,
with temperature variant;
costal lives in danger, wrath of anger of hurricane,
weather completely insane;
Furious winds plucking off,
everything on their quest;
thirsty typhoon's cuff,
snapping up lives in their chest;
Giving all a sore feet,
quintessence of death;
death's meet,
essence of bloody path;
Stay in your cocoon,
during the hour of cyclone;
everything will be alright soon,
you're not alone;
The day will definitely arrive, with the moon's light!

# 44. The superior

what is greatness?

is it own the splendours wealth?

is it to be master of constant health?

is it about being ruler?

or the triumph of never being a failure;

The great Alexander,

on the verge of his death,

he couldn't find a cure,

which could hold his life lure;

The great Ashoka,

victorious of Kalinga battle,

letting off all his desires,

changed himself into innocence of the cattle;

During his last breath, Alexander

asked his sculptor to carve a coffin for him;

hands stretched out, portraying "he conquered the whole world,

inevitable from the death's fold";

Neither being ferocious, nor being atrocious

will get you to the world's zenith, dear

the moment you let go off all the fear,

wisdom will be the colour on your face, which you will smear!

# 45. Inheritance

Inheritance;
a pinch of sweetfull essence,
tales of legacy, is it's presence;
You are it's bearer in the time to commence;
Respect forged by them,
am I capable to carry them?
How? the question of hem
answer is in you not in them;
You can be that unique bird,
in the unique world;
Or the one with wings of dust,
with nothing in your chest;
Foreseen fostered ice,
may burn you like spice;
Adapting yourself for a goal,
will never make you pay a toll;
hey beautiful soul,
you can make the best;
Your goal,
will make your legacy boast;

# 46. Enemy behind the drapes

Blunders by wars,

fired up cars,

flowing blood from scars,

and enemy is not from mars;

Brother next door,

bloodshot gun roar,

profoundly established political fear,

families, lives, economies tear;

Syria, Iraq, Iran, Afghanistan: geopolitical crisis,

their own established nationality infringes upon

compromises;

war is between two,

but the master is the Big daddy! you know who;

Give them arms,

and pledge to protect the world from harm,

pose to be a savour,

and harness the terror?

What a game to fetch free resources,

to establish themselves as power sources,

stamping countries to dust and loot,

sew the scar on the name of 'peace' hem;

Building up power vacuum,

for the terrorist and poverty to bloom;
Is this the game of power?
or for the money scour;
Nevertheless,
Many world power may boil their food in others blood,
Nationality and unity must be strong as wood,
only a good leader can distinguish between
a holy saviour and a bloody terror!

# 47. Misinterpretation

Sometimes things you speak

may pierce the heart at a peak,

why so eloquent

it was just some random rubbish of the moment;

You cry again and again

thinking of the same vain,

which was lame

and still you are the same;

Agrhh! why brain why you misinterpret

you are the culprit,

for my pain

for my bloody gain;

my brain is guilty

but your heart is mighty,

hold me back

let me shack;

Give me misery

my brain deserves it,

make me weary

like a burtout fire pit;

My foolish cocksureness

still your harness,

I am full of fuss

you can cuss;
Heart, forgive his dumb brain
it's thinner than tane,
forget this insane
hold me back my mane;

# 48. lone

When you are stuck in the storm of loneliness,

never think you are alone;

When you can't find your own lost soul,

it will flux, not your foul;

Never ever whine,

that you are not wealthy enough to have wine;

indeed there are ample things to make you feel completely
fine,

Never be proud about your badges,

because in this journey you have to face many ambages;

Never let the fire in you expiate,

indeed let it deflagrate;

test yourself before you detest

you are not lone,

you are with your soul!

# 49. Star and me.

• 64 •

O stars, you are again shining
pushed the dark doom of clouds without whining
I am glad "dearest star, you came on the chariot of night"
fighting the hitches gallantly with all might;
You came to look into my eye,
spreading the sparkle in the sky;
caressing my cheeks, making me shy,
"revive your seldom sensation of seduction again, please try"!
You brought the blush in me by your bliss,
dear stars, freckles on the cheeks of sky, bless
the serenity of your beauty with a soft kiss;
Yes my star yes, you made me sort from the mess;
Star you are my companion in this peaceful night,
Gratias! you gave me intense pleasure just by your sight!

# 50. Mother!

With all the pain
she is dripping by the heat, clutching the sheets,
her body feels numb contentment in her moan,
pain repeats, repeats and repeats
alas! fisting her might
through the fire and ice fight,
there was this tiniest life glowing bright;
a blossom of bliss struggling its own fright!
A child crawling in her bosom
She is nurturing the elements of nature for its nourishment,
looking at his growth her eyes were numm
she was ready to elude all her elite essence for his
encouragement;
How can he try to wipe off her presence?
her bounties of beauty will be bursting into fumes in the time
to commence;
compassion which grew in her womb,
is now trying to blast her with his destructive bomb;
The essence of the world is in extinction,
Purity is perishing with pollution,
destruction with various dimension
life on the sphere of persecution;

For his act he will repent for sure,

he thought by destruction he would rule,

dumped her in the trash,

she made his survival harsh.

She is flooding

She is drying up

She is flying off

and she is bursting off

For your deeds,

you will lose the mother who feeds,

for your behaviour,

you will see Satan in your saviour;

She is our mother

how can we not bother she gave us everything,

now it's our responsibility to make her a healthy forever thing!!